W9-DAS-402

WHAT HAPPY WOMEN DO

To my sisters Lynn, Kelly, Jenny and Michelle and, of course, my BFFsters
Molly, Deb, Bets, Deborah, Trish and Sarah: you fill me up.
—Carol

To the women with whom I share ugly faces, taco dip, pearls,
and butter toast: our laughter inspires me every day.
—Anna

Nail Night and the Unicorn Dance

WHAT HAPPY WOMEN DO

A Salute to Sisterhood and the Rituals That Sustain Us

Carol J. Bruess, Ph.D., & Anna D.H. Kudak, M.A.

WHAT HAPPY WOMEN DO © 2010 by Carol J. Bruess and Anna D.H. Kudak. All rights reserved.

Published by Fairview Press, 2450 Riverside Avenue, Minneapolis, Minnesota 55454. Fairview Press is a division of Fairview Health Services, a community-focused health system, affiliated with the University of Minnesota. For a free current catalog of Fairview Press titles, please call toll-free 1-800-544-8207. Or visit our Web site at www.fairviewpress.org.

Library of Congress Cataloging-in-Publication Data
Bruess, Carol J., 1968-
 What happy women do : nail night and the unicorn dance—a salute to sisterhood and the rituals that sustain us / by Carol J. Bruess, Anna D. H. Kudak.
    p. cm.
 ISBN 978-1-57749-233-7 (alk. paper)
 1. Female friendship. 2. Interpersonal relations. 3. Women—Psychology. I. Kudak, Anna D. H., 1982- II. Title.
 BF575.F66B78 2010
 177.62082—dc22

                    2010005701

Printed in China
First Printing: 2010
14 13 12 11 10   5 4 3 2 1

Interior design by Natalie Nowytski, Renaissance Jane,
      and Ryan Scheife, Mayfly Design (www.mayflydesign.net)
Cover illustration by Scott Andre

Share Your Stories

If you are inspired by the stories in this book and have your own rituals to share, please tell us about them.

Visit **www.whathappycouplesdo.com** and click on *Share Your Stories*. We would love to hear what you are DOing to create sisterness. We also invite you to share stories of rituals involving other relationships in your life—with your spouse, family, children, co-workers, whomever. Or simply e-mail us:

Carol Bruess and Anna Kudak
carol&anna@whathappycouplesdo.com

Introduction

Who are *your* "sisters"? Those women in your life you have given the honorific title of "sister"? Your best girlfriend. Your female soul mate. Your "sistah." Sometimes, it's even your actual sister. No matter their source, *sisters* are the women we lean on, call on, and who show up when we need them most. True *sisters*? They share an unshakable loyalty.

Happy and healthy women in the 21st century intuitively know, deep in their bones, that meaningful and deeply personal relationships with their *sisters* are essential to their well-being. Yes, we adore and rely on our children, partners, and spouses. But we yearn in a unique way for uninterrupted listen-to-what-I-just-heard-I-can't-believe-my-boss/husband/kid-just-said-that-oh-my-gosh time with our *sisters*. But why? Is there something unparalleled about the bond of women? Indeed there is. And there's actually a bit of contemporary science behind this centuries-old relationship and how it contributes to our *being* well.

Quite simply: Close female friendships make us healthier and happier. Help us feel better. Serve as stress reduction. Especially as we get older (Fox, Gibbs, & Auerbach, 2006). In fact, the more friends a woman has as she ages, the less likely she is to suffer serious and significant health problems over time (Taylor et al., 2000). And—believe it or not—the same group of researchers who uncovered the health-friendship connection report that *lack* of close female relationships is as bad for your health as cigarettes and obesity. Sisters, we're serious.

In *What Happy Women Do*, we explore both the science and the art of the best-female-friend connection. We do so by sharing the stories of more than 50 sets of *sisters* and their sometimes silly, often heartwarming, and always-inspiring rituals of connection. In their own words, women from all over the country, of all ages and stages, share what they DO to create and sustain signature sisterness. And how such relationships are what see them through life. For when you have *sisters*, you cannot be defeated. Not by death, cancer, or conflict. Not by job loss, family feuds, or fledgling children. So, what's the secret to sustaining strong sistership?

Sisters DO things that keep them emotionally and symbolically connected. They develop silly little rituals. Share in large and small moments, escapes, gatherings, and traditions of both mundane and great significance. They also create nicknames and code words, and can finish each other's thoughts and sentences. Women—through their rituals—travel similar paths and know deeply that no matter the journey, their sisters will pave the way when the terrain is rocky, celebrate milestones with unabashed and selfless enthusiasm, and offer guidance at life's many crossroads. And *sisters* DO so time and again, with a sense of purpose and pride.

We've surveyed and interviewed women about their sister bonds for the sole purpose of inspiring you to salute those same women in your life. To intentionally and mindfully care for these crucial and substantial relationships. And—whether quietly or exuberantly, whatever your style—to celebrate them.

Do you fully embrace and appreciate the women in your life? How DO you make sure you secure and sustain the bonds of female friends? Allow the stories within to instruct and inspire. For the tales told by the women in this book take us inside the human relationship we females know is—simply—quite fabulous: sisterhood.

The Jacket

" A few years ago, my sisters and I visited our parents in Florida. We were shopping together when my oldest sister, Marilyn, tried on a jacket that we all just loved. Since we each have the same coloring—strawberry blond hair, light complexion—we knew that whatever color looked good on one of us would look good on all of us. Plus, we don't live in the same cities or even in the same states, so we knew we could all buy the same jacket and never embarrass each other showing up at the same event looking alike. The next year, we all went to celebrate our mother's 85th birthday, and we bought one of the jackets for her so she could be part of our 'club.' On my dad's 86th birthday, we all wore them for his birthday celebration. The jackets took on a life of their own! After a couple of years, my younger sister found another jacket that looked stunning on her and sent us each one for a special occasion. Now, *we will sometimes let each other know when we're wearing it so we can wear it on the same day and think of each other. And we have family celebrations where we all wear 'the jacket.' It's been wonderful fun and has made us feel special together.* "

Whatever the season or the reason, sisters seem to inherently know that symbolic connection—be it in language, action, or wardrobe—is not only wonderful fun but wonderfully functional as well. When we create our own "miniculture" (Wood, 1982) of jackets, hats, tattoos, or (don't tell) nicknames for our husbands, we celebrate the shared reality of our special sisterhoods and we reinforce, like the sisters in this story, the irreplaceable bonds.

What do you DO with your sisters, or best friends, to celebrate your one-of-a-kind relationship?

Celebrate

THE SHARED REALITY
OF YOUR
SISTERNESS.

Super Triple
Double-Dutch

"*When my sister and I were little we made up a special way of saying goodnight to my parents. 'I love you, good night' wasn't enough. We always would say, 'I love you super, triple, double-Dutch, forever, ever, ever.' And that's what we'd say every night before we went to bed. And we'd say it to each other too. It was funny because you could tell Lisa was the older and more creative of the two of us because she came up with 'super, triple, double-Dutch.' And all I could add on was, 'forever, ever, ever.' So . . . that's what we would say every night. I think it's so cute. Now it will come up if we write a birthday card or send each other mail or e-mails.*"

Seriously, when it comes to our sisters, most of us would agree that they center us, forever and ever, double-triple-super-duper-can't-imagine-what-to-do-without-them. No? And like these sisters, most of us have found ways to elaborately, or at least frequently, express our adoration for the women in our lives because we know that even if our expressions are corny or ooey-gooey-double-Dutchy, our gal pals fill a sweet spot in our lives.

Have you told the important women in your life lately how much you adore them super-triple-a-lot?

This "Ugly" Game

" My friends and I have been playing a modified version of this game since we were in our early teens. One day my best friend and I were sitting on my bathroom counter goofing off. We'd turn our heads around, count to three, and when we'd turn back around to face each other, we'd have contorted our faces in some odd, ugly way. Then we'd laugh and laugh at each other's 'ugly' faces. In high school we modified the game. We'd make an ugly face and ask each other, 'Would you still be my friend if I looked like this?' Then we'd adapt it to our environment and with our larger group of friends, too: for instance, at a dance we'd do a really crazy move and ask, 'Would you still be my friend if I danced like this?' It makes us laugh so hard. We've been playing this 'ugly' game for nearly 15 years. "

Women of all ages report that female friendship is grounded in a gorgeous feeling of trust. When women are asked to describe their friendships they, according to Ellen Goodman and Patricia O'Brien, authors of *I Know Just What You Mean: The Power of Friendship in Women's Lives* (2000), are more apt to proclaim the *impact* of their friendships than simply describe their qualities: "being known and accepted, understood to the core; feeling you can count on trust and loyalty, having someone on your side; having someone to share worries and secrets as well as the good stuff of life, someone who needs you in return."

Women's friendships are beautiful because they allow our true selves to emerge: the good, the bad, and the "ugly." Without evaluation. Without retaliation. Whenever. However.

In Friendship
Our True Self
Is Embraced.
Is Encouraged.
IS EMERGED.

4   I Saved My Dicky

❝ Long ago my sister, Becky, and I got matching dickies (you know, those fake little turtlenecks) for Christmas. Being that it was the height of our Goth/metal/grunge era, circa 1994, it didn't really fit into our wardrobes. But for some reason I saved my dicky. And then when our mom called one year to announce that Becky was going to be graduating from NYU, I decided to send her a present. What better than a dicky stuffed into a Tampax box? And so it began. The dicky has made its way over miles and years, in and out of our lives and homes, in the most unexpected ways. Once my sister totally dogged me with it at the last second before I was leaving for Europe for a semester. As I was walking down the ramp to board my plane she called out to me with a 'good-bye' present, which of course I ran back to get! Once on the *plane I opened the box and realized that I was stuck with the dicky for three months. I vowed at that very moment to get revenge.*

So, I continued to save the dicky until my sister's first baby shower; I stuffed that thing in a box with Minnie Mouse. Her friends weren't very amused by our dicky story, but we both knew I totally got her! In vain, she put it into a coffee machine that was my Christmas present the next year. The dicky is still out there right now. Where is it?! I'm sure I'll find out soon."

Although irreplaceable, sisterhood is not immune to erosion. Like all satisfying relationships, sisters who consciously stay close sustain secrets, games, and rituals of connection. They DO things to stay close, repeatedly shoring up the bond that has—like it or not—made an indelible stamp on their identities.

Clap-Clap-Stomp

My best girlfriends and I have a little sign we use to indicate that we think someone handsome, like a cute guy, is walking by. We 'Clap-Clap-Stomp'. . . two claps followed by a little stomp. It's our own sign that we can do anywhere and anytime.

For decades, relationship researchers have studied the way private language bonds members of close relationships. Like romantic couples, friends and sisters who develop their own "language" through gestures, words, or signals are also developing a sense of "we-ness." Private codes, like a clap or stomp, not only allow us efficient communication but also help create a "culture of two" (or three or four!).

What language or gestures do you and your best girlfriends or sisters share? Whatever its form, protect it. Over time, it's the little symbolic moments that will defend your relationship from dissolution as well.

EMBRACE THE SENSE OF

WE-NESS

ONLY YOU AND YOUR

Sistahs

KNOW.

Remembering Cathe

A little more than five years ago, a dear friend from college, Catherine, died after an on-again, off-again battle (she called it 'inconvenient') with breast cancer for years. She was 49. Her little boy was 11. It broke our hearts.

Cathe had a way of collecting friends like some people collect coins. She polished all of us and scooped us together in a pile. Lo and behold, we became friends, good friends who gather several times a year to flirt with Italian waiters, eat too much, and drink a bunch of wine. Sometimes we top it off with a forbidden cigarette, just because Cathe liked being a bit of a rebel.

After she died we had a tree planted in her honor on the campus of her alma mater, St. Catherine University in St. Paul, Minnesota. Each spring it boasts pink blooms, and a bench now graces the site, too. On July 31, the anniversary of her death, I sit there again, drinking in a kind of silence almost antithetical to Cathe's nature: She was Irish and never shut up, except sometimes in church, and even then she usually found something to whisper and giggle about.

As I sit there thinking about Cathe, I hope there is, indeed, the afterlife to which we Christians cling. I have some good gossip I need to tell her and I need to feel again the special kind of exhaustion that endless laughter brings. I need her to tell me a story. I miss her 'cackle.'

Last July 31, my reverie was interrupted. Someone walking to his car after a campus summer music conference had burst into a perfect-pitch rendition of 'Amazing Grace.' Thanks, Cathe.

As William Shakespeare once aptly said, "A ministering angel shall my sister be."

M&M Club

"   After my friends and I graduated from high school our moms planned a monthly movie night to fill the void of their missing daughters. They call it M & M, which stands for moms and movies, but it could be called Triple M because they get malts at a diner afterward, too. For nearly eight years they've been doing this. Here are the rules, which they tell us about all the time: They never pick a movie beforehand; they just go to the theater and pick once they get there. They have a set pattern of who shares malts, and who shares fries, based on who likes their fries crispy and who likes them softer, and who likes strawberry malts and who likes chocolate. When it is time to leave they have a group hug. If it is someone's birthday that month they sing to that person. They have a rotation of who will coordinate the day they'll all go the next month. They also keep a journal of which movie they saw, when *their birthdays are, and how each mom rated it (1–5), and they tape one ticket stub to that page. They can almost predict how each other will rate movies (one mom always rates them low and one always high).* "

What's the *deal* with the female friendship bond? We all know it's fun. It's free therapy. We enjoy it. And most of us have many such bonds because—gosh darn it—they make us feel good. But did you know there is science behind the "good" feelings we get from our favorite female friendships?

In a series of fascinating studies, scientists reveal that close female friendships can actually counteract the negative effects of stress on our physical health. Especially as we age. According to the authors of *Healthy Women, Healthy Lives: A Guide to Preventing Disease from the Landmark Nurses' Health Study* (Hankinson et al., 2001), the more friends a woman has the more likely she is to report being "joyful" and the less likely she is to suffer serious and significant health problems over time. The results of the studies are so profound that the researchers conclude that lack of close female friends is as bad for your health as smoking and being overweight.

Next time you head out for that cherished ritual with your "sisters," take heart knowing that Harvard researchers are cheering you on!

A Poignant Equation:

FEMALES

+

FRIENDSHIP

=

Health & Happiness.

A Commanding Day

"For the last 40 years my friend from college and I write to each other on March 4th. It started as a silly, private joke between us: 'What is the only day of the year that gives a command?' Answer: 'March 4th (forth).' The year after graduation, Meg wrote to me just to remind me of the joke, and I wrote back, and then we got into the habit of writing every year to catch up on events. In 40 years we have only seen each other maybe four or five times, but I know I can expect a letter from Meg—with good news, bad news, and all the news in between—every March 4th."

Our relationships need maintenance. Like any other well-functioning aspects of our lives—cars, finances, and calendars—we must give our relationships a bit of ongoing attention and nourishment.

The magic of rituals, like the annual letter writing of these friends, is that no matter their shape, size, or frequency, they provide equilibrium and imply a future. Because of their rich symbolic value, rituals remind us of our history while propelling our sisterness into the years ahead.

Rituals of connection clearly strengthen and sustain relationships. What are you doing to maintain yours?

My Sister Roo

" My sister is biological but we were not raised together. I was adopted and thus we grew up across the country from each other without knowing the other existed. When I got married I decided to do a search for my birth mother. I found her and was told that I had three siblings: a sister and two brothers. I was so excited to meet everyone! Soon I learned that my sister had moved to my home state, Minnesota, for college and we were living two miles apart! We met and there was an immediate bond between us; she quickly became and is still my closest friend. For some reason I started calling her Roo and bought her, for one of her birthdays, a little stuffed Roo from Winnie-the-Pooh. She has kept that little Roo with her ever since. Even though our lives have gotten quite busy between her career and my kids, Roo will often stop by after *work and sit with me and my three girls. We'll open a bottle of wine and laugh like no time has passed.*

To have a sister and best friend like Roo—which we bet you have in some form, too—is to have a sisterly soul mate. DO make sure not too much time passes before letting her know the special place she has in your life.

Her heart will sing "ya-hoo!"

A Sister is a Gift
to the *Heart,*
a Friend to the Spirit,
a Golden Thread
to the Meaning of Life.

—ISADORA JAMES

10 Got Wedding?

My sisters and I always spend at least part of our summer vacation at our family cabin. And one thing we always do before we go is buy tons of wedding magazines. None of us is engaged but every summer we go ahead and plan our weddings, picking out dresses, rings, hairdos, and bridesmaid dresses!

With whom else can we imagine our futures, live in our present moments, and plan for the guests, garish up-dos, and gory details of parties that exist only in our great imaginations? With our sisters, that's who. Our girlfriends. Our best friends.

What do you and your sisters and friends look forward to DOing at least once a year? That only you can appreciate and understand?

Your relationships are, quite simply, what you make them. Invest in them, for they are priceless, indeed.

Your Relationships Are What You Make Them. *Invest in Them.* They are Priceless.

11 Never!

I have five sisters. My mom always said, 'You girls will grow up to be best friends.' We would turn up our noses and think, 'Never!' But my mom was right. We are an inseparable group of six best friends who happen to be sisters.

Today, as adults, we always show up when one of us needs something. We travel in a pack and provide insulation for each other. As kids, my sisters and I would kneel together in the hallway each night before we went to bed and say the rosary. We were inspired by the deep faith of my parents, and faith is what held us together. Today, oftentimes, just the six of us will meet at church to say some prayers.

We also have unstoppable fun as a sister six-pack. For instance, our family festivities are never complete without a T-shirt for all to commemorate the event. We have girls-only two-week camping trips every summer. We have a Sisters-Going-Home trip to the place we grew up, sisters' getaways, '6 Sisters' annual garage sales, 'Sisters Only' outings to play craps (a skill our parents taught us), our traditional Poinsettia Punch (about which, every year, our mom would say, 'There isn't much alcohol in here, is there, girls?' to which we just smile and say, 'Cheers!'). We end the year with our annual 'Sisters' Christmas dinner.'

I look to my older sisters for advice and I look to my younger sisters to keep me hip. My sisters are my rock and a consistent constant in my life. Together we are quite a package. "

Who forms the bountiful package of rock-hip-advice-providing goodness in your life? If nonexistent or simply not as rock-solid consistent as you'd like it to be, DO something right now to begin making your sisterness bonds stronger. Tighter. Something you'd commemorate, over and forever.

Together,
Sisters are Rocks.
A Consistent
Constant
in our Lives.

Nail Night

A group of my favorite 'sistahs' and I started 'nail night.' It's grown to include about 12 of the greatest gals around. My friend, a professional chef, hosts nail night about once a month. We all bring wine. We hire a pedicurist. And we show up for great conversation, a little destressing, a manicure and/or pedicure, and great food, of course.

When friends get together for nail night, movie night, or just time away from their children, partners, or external pressures, they are doing what researchers call "tending and befriending" (Taylor et al., 2000). According to researchers like Shelley Taylor and her colleagues at UCLA, women's friendship reduces the stress hormones in our bodies, providing a healthful sense of calm. In her research on stress and female friendship, Taylor and her co-researchers found that stressed women release oxytocin, the hormone traditionally known to help mothers bond with their newborns. Oxytocin in stressed female bodies is now believed also to encourage females to build strong friendships with other women, which, in turn, help ward off the harmful effects of stress.

If you're still not convinced that female friendships are empirically good for us, cite this simple fact the next time someone complains that you're spending too much time with your sisters or friends: female friendship might be precisely why women live longer than men (and longer than women who lack strong intimate or social connections). Nail night, anyone?

I'm Thinking Tuna

"*I lived with four friends in college. Living in a big old house and sharing chores and only one bathroom, we definitely became sisters. Since then, we have a really big can of tuna we pass amongst the five of us every once in a while. Many of us used to eat tuna almost daily during college, despite warnings from our mothers about mercury poisoning. One wild night, we thought it would be funny to steal a huge can of tuna from the kitchen of another friend. The best line of that night: 'This could feed us for months!' Of course, none of us has had the heart to open and eat it because of the memories it provides. Instead, every year or so we'll slip it into one of our cars, a purse, or leave it where you least expect to find it. It comes with a note: 'This could feed us for months!'"*

Humans desire laughter. It feeds our imaginations. Lowers our blood pressure. Heightens our mood. Nourishes our creativity. Enlivens our souls. And among female friends, fun and playfulness are like icing on the cake of an already enriching relationship.

If something special has diminished or vanished from your relationship, DO something to get it back again. Maybe begin anew an old yet playful ritual, one reminding you and your friends how great relationships feed us. For months. For years. Forever and ever.

Playfulness

IS THE *ICING*

on the Cake

OF *Friendship.*

14 Pie Party

I have 11 girlfriends who have been developing a strong and lasting friendship since junior high school, more than 35 years ago. One thing we do to stay connected now is all go to one of the girls' cabin for a weekend. It's called the 'Pie Party Weekend.' Even though we usually don't eat pie, the name lives on because one time when we were in high school we had an actual Pie Party. Everyone brought a different kind of pie. We ate and indulged. As time went on, we had dessert parties and salad parties, but the name 'Pie Party' seemed to stick. Today, through many of life's good and hard times, our lasting friendship with our very best friends—the women we know will all be there for one another, no matter what—endures.

When all else fails in our lives, our lasting and best friendships endure.
No matter how you slice it. French silk or lemon meringue. The women in
your life will be there for you.

15 Oh, Crap, What Number?

"One of the biggest things we get about each other is how much our sore throats can bring us to our knees. In all my life there have only been a couple of people who really feel the same way. We quickly began a ranking system so that the other person would know exactly how bad the sore throat is. On a scale of 1–10 with 1 being, 'I can tell it's coming, it's just a matter of time,' to 10, which is 'I'd rather be dead.' We're now at the point where we can just call and if one of us sounds sorta sick, the other one just says, 'Oh, crap, what number?' It is also understood that we will be checking in on each other in a day or two. 'What number now?'"

Isn't it priceless when you have that friend in your life who simply knows what you mean? No elaborate explanations necessary. No unnecessary explications required.

As the authors of *I Just Know What You Mean: The Power of Friendship in Women's Lives* describe, when women speak of their connections with other women, they refer to the same phrase over and over: Our best girlfriends simply "just know what I mean." That, my friends, summarizes the power of female relationships in our lives.

TALK BUILDS GREAT

Friendships.

KNOWING WHAT SHE MEANS
BEFORE SHE EVEN SAYS IT:

EVEN BETTER.

16 My Person

"*My sugar pie, my honey pie, my sweetie pie is not my husband. No. She's my girl. My person. The one I tell everything and the one for whom and to whom, I listen. The one I call to say some quick thing that lasts an hour. We use pet names a lot. They've become somewhat of a code, signaling mood, health, even time of day. And the absence of its use means something else altogether. Although such names are typically reserved for a significant other, she is the epitome of everything that a husband simply can't be. Nor should he be. And thankfully our respective (and respectful) husbands are grateful not to be the 'only' one. Besides, my husband calls me 'buns.' And that's totally different.*"

What's totally different about women's friendships is that they are, indeed, the epitome of everything good. Everything a relationship can and should be.

Even when they challenge and concern us, the precious and forever friendship will emerge brighter. Unscathed. Ready for another decade and more listening. Signaling. Coding. Respecting. Chitchatting (and then some). All times of the day and about every topic imaginable.

Who's your "person"?

17 The Tower Girls

" *Age, like a good wine, improves friendships over time. But sometimes it creates new ones altogether. My parents moved into a retirement facility a few years ago. While my mother still maintains her friendships outside of the 'Towers,' she has created a new network of 'girls' with whom to bond. Most of the women are widows, some are not. All have aches and pains and stories to tell. Three years into her residency, Mom created a 'therapy group' for herself and her friends. Not PT, OT, or RT. Simply girls' 'talk time' therapy. No husbands, doctors, or care providers. Just four women having lunch every Tuesday, sharing the woes, the joys, and the news of their lives. Sometimes they grieve together, sometimes they gossip, but always they gather and create a time and a place for each other. Long live the friendships of women.* "

What else can we say? Long live the friendships of women, indeed.

Long Live
The Friendships
Of Women.

Seriously Oscar-Worthy

" *My friend of over 15 years and I go see a movie every one or two weeks, trying to see only seriously Oscarworthy movies. We both love to be on top of what actors are hot, what movies are hot, etc. And let's not kid ourselves, movies provide a great escape. So we meet a little early and get one large popcorn and one large lemonade to share. Before or after the movie we exchange hand-me-downs, books to read, and of course parenting stories/advice. Sometimes we even get in a little shopping. It's so important for us to get out during the week and leave the kid stuff—homework, dinner, bedtimes—to the dads. We then celebrate our year's worth of movies by watching the Oscars! But of course we don't watch it together because a Sunday night with kids makes it nearly impossible to actually get together for this big event. Instead, we e-mail or call back and forth the entire time during the show to express our strong feelings about who got the award and, even more important, what the stars are wearing.*

Seriously worthy friends are those who make the effort—time and again—to leave all else behind and celebrate their shared interests. They also make sure to prioritize and share the large, small, dramatic, Oscar-esque and oh-so-mundane aspects of each other's daily lives. The day-to-day is what makes a friendship (drum roll, please) award-worthy.

19

My Ya-Yas

About 10 years ago I took the plunge and left my career and the safety of a dual income. It was time for me to try my hand at being a stay-at-home mom. It was terrifying! My biggest fear was wondering, 'How would I meet other moms?' Friendships and being social are EVERYTHING to me!

My fear was unfounded. After joining a baby/mom exercise class, I met my 'Ya-Ya' sisters. We are six strong women who come from all walks of life. We are Republican, Democrat, divorced, parents of both adopted and biological children, Italian and Irish. Our mission in life is to raise happy and healthy children. Our children brought us together, but our spirits, humor, and need for each other made us 'sisters.'

The Ya-Yas have done many 'girl' trips, our most memorable one being to a remote Georgia island. And we are always planning our next trip. It doesn't matter if we are on a beautiful, warm tropical beach or a cabin in frigid northern Minnesota. Because we could be anyplace and find something funny to laugh about. The Ya-Yas have been through some rough times, too. We have struggled through a divorce, cancer, depression, financial uncertainty, learning issues with children, you name it. Friends weave in and out of your life but the Ya-Yas will endure.

Whatever your struggles, your truest "sisters" will weave their way into your soul. And then be there for the duration.

20

You into Unicorns?

"*For many decades my best friend, Heather, and I have shared an ongoing ritual that began way back in junior high. For some reason we made up a 'unicorn dance' that we have continued to execute nearly every time we are together, even now that we are grown adults! We used to and continue to write notes to each other and sign them 'Uni-Heather' or 'Uni-Donna.' And although we don't see each other as much anymore, we ALWAYS continue our unicorn dance tradition every time we see each other. Recently, for instance, when I went to the airport to pick her up after she had been overseas for an entire year, the minute I saw her in the baggage claim area she broke into the unicorn dance for me and then ran my way for a big hug. Today, we just laugh at how dumb we were to think of this in the first place, yet we also love how it continues to connect us.*"

Why leave the imaginative play to the kids? Research shows that play in adulthood is just as important for both our mental and physical health. And a huge bonus for relationships. Besides, who cares how precisely ridiculous you look when you do your uni-que dance or strut your uni-que self. It will continue to uni-quely enhance your friendship—and your mood—no doubt. Uni-eed any more encouragement?

KEEP YOUR Sisterhoods *Alive* WITH MOMENTARY silliness.

All Acts
Of Positivity
Will be
Reciprocated
In Myriad Ways.

21
A Waitress? Not Really

" *My best friend and I share the same color of toenail polish: the color by OPI called 'Not Really a Waitress.' It's the brightest, shiny red. We often will call and say, 'Are you a waitress?' or 'I'm not really a waitress today. You?' Or when talking about careers, kids, decisions, life—the stuff we talk about pretty much nonstop— we'll say out of the blue: 'You could be a waitress.' Or 'Maybe you ARE a waitress.' I laugh the hardest when we use it to remind our husbands, friends, and each other: 'I'm NOT really a waitress today.'* "

Our best girlfriends, those precious few upon whom we bestow the honorary title "sister," are relationships built in the everyday moments. The stuff of talk—a mixture of serious and seriously out of the blue—which not only reflects who we are but actually helps create our sense of self.

Whether you're a waitress, seamstress, endocrinologist, or journalist, your true sisters bring out the very brightest and shiniest in you.

YOUR *True Sisters*
BRING OUT
the Brightest and
Shiniest IN YOU.

22

Fresh Pajamas

" On Christmas Eve, my sisters and I all gather around the Christmas tree with great anticipation for a gift we get every year: a new pair of pajamas, given to us by our parents, to wear to bed that night! They are always the same pajamas but in different variations . . . Julie might get blue pants, me red, and Carla green. Or one might have pigs, one cats, and one penguins. It's always so fun to go to bed in fresh new PJs and wake up in them—with my sisters—on Christmas morning! And no matter how old we get, we will still do this. "

The bonds that begin in our childhoods can be immensely gratifying . . . and ever-lasting! If you've let go of an old tradition because you think you're too old, why not try it on again for size and see if it might still fit? No PJs (necessarily) required.

WHATEVER LIFE BRINGS
YOUR SISTERS WILL
Pick you up.
Prop you up.
Keep you going.

23

Knucklehead

"*Four of my favorite female friends and I started our Knucklehead tradition 15 years ago with a trip to Door County, Wisconsin. Lisa, one of the Knuckleheads, told her husband that she should start her own Knucklehead getaway just like he had been doing for many years with his college buddies; they had always called themselves the Knuckleheads. And so we did and we called it Knucklehead too, of course. One of us always 'takes charge' to plan the next outing. It involves picking the spot and making travel and hotel arrangements. We try to do one every year. However, since we can't afford to travel big all the time, every other year we go to my cousin's cottage, which is within driving distance of where most of us live. Over the years we've been to Las Vegas, New York, Boston, the Berkshires, San Francisco, and Chicago.*

While on a Knuckle, there is much shopping. We've even had to put on a car top carrier in anticipation of purchases. And it did get filled up. If there is a spa around, we find it. If there is a casino around, we go for an hour or two. There is one absolute rule on Knuckle: We always stick together. No one goes off on her own. Ever. We usually spend most of our time talking; we've been known to skip meals if we're into a good conversation. Why do we love it? History. No judgments. Therapy. Time away from our husbands and kids. Confidence booster. No matter what we're going through, Knuckles will love you and support you.

So, what are you waiting for, knucklehead? Gather your best buds. Give your group a name. Go away. Talk. Create history. Avoid judging. Build each other up. And then love and sustain your tradition like the original Knuckles do: For the therapy. The break. The memories. And the judgment-free conversation.

Sign us up!

24 Yo Mama

"Clare was my mentor in my first job in New York City. She's about 65 and has a very gruff and tough exterior: Brooklyn accent, Mets fan, street smart navigator of New York on the fewest nickels possible, lives in a rough neighborhood, etc. But, she's really the kindest soul you could know, once you crack the tough exterior. Clare even gave the homily at our wedding. So I've made a commitment to take each of my girls to NYC for a solo weekend with Mom and Clare. I have done three of these weekends with one to go. She gives up her time to ride the subways all around with us, do the Staten Island Ferry, make her famous chocolate raisin brownies, elbow her way through Chinatown, and she really tries to toughen up my midwestern kids so they're not 'soft.' So despite all the other great vacation options, *and despite the challenges of being little in a giant, chaotic city like New York, my kids always list that as the place they want to see again, but only if Clare's there. And only if they can hear her shout 'Yo Mama' to someone littering outside her brownstone.*

Yo, sisters and fiercely fabulous female friends: Consider the way the women in your life are a substantial influence in the lives of your own children. If not substantial enough—because of time or distance or effort or energy—when exactly do you think such will be plentiful? DO something to ensure your children will have the chances you have to be inspired by all the great women in your life.

25

She and I Plan

" My sister, Sheila, and I have a tradition at our annual large family get-together at a lake in August. One of us plans a gigantic scavenger hunt with three multigenerational teams. Our family is widely known as being very quiet people, but when it comes down to it, we're very, very competitive. So the scavenger hunt is complicated, and it involves driving to nearby towns for hidden clues, deciphering code, rowing out to the middle of the lake to retrieve objects, calling around the country to get answers to arcane family trivia, collecting live specimens, and so on. The one who organizes it stays 'on campus' with the littlest kids, acts as judge, and hands out prizes. It usually takes about an hour for each team to get done and it's always a photo finish (for some reason). The rules are that you have to obey all traffic rules and the whole team has to find each answer/clue together; that is, you can't send X *off to get this and Y off to get that to be more efficient. Sheila and I have an unspoken agreement that we can push the competition only so far, just short of where people's darker natures take over.*

Research is quite conclusive: Women are the kinkeepers of families (Leach & Braithwaite, 1996). They create and sustain traditions. They bring folks together. They push us toward competitions, opportunities, and histories. They push us toward each other in valuable and precious ways.

What can you and your sisters DO to bring out the brightest side of your close or extended family? You might just find the unexpected and most valuable outcome is the camaraderie you feel with each other as you co-create a generation-crossing-push-the-cousins-to-their-limits competition or contest.

Let the planning begin.

Women
Are the Kin
Who Bring
Folks
Together.

26

Texas Grapefruits

My great college friend, Missy, absolutely loved watching ice-skating competitions on TV; she'd get out a TV tray, cut open a grapefruit with a special grapefruit knife, sprinkle sugar on it, put on her huge Alvin and the Chipmunks slippers, and settle in front of the TV. So the Winter Olympics were the absolute best time for her. She'd get her work done way in advance to watch them every night. I never cared a bit about ice-skating or the Winter Olympics until I met her. But from then on, it was a great bonding experience. Even after college when we lived very far apart, we'd chat on the phone once a week. When she was 35, Missy died of brain cancer, leaving a husband and son. Among the many ways I try to remember and honor her is to carve out time for plenty of ice-skating on TV (even when other things are pressing), and I eat

Texas grapefruits using a special knife a couple of times a week during the winter, as do my kids, and they know why. "

Who else but a true "sister" would notice the special knife you covet or the character slippers you cherish?

DO honor your sisters. For they will do the same for you, paying homage to all that makes you precisely *you.*

PAY HOMAGE TO ALL THAT MAKES YOUR *Sister* PRECISELY WHO SHE IS.

27

Now Go

" *I like to tell my best friend that when she gets Alzheimer's she'll finally be like the rest of us. Because although I like to think that I have a good memory, her recall of detail is truly amazing and is one of the many lovely ways that she attends to others, in addition to the general aura of sunshine around her. A typical check-in after a holiday spent with relatives will have her telling her stories at a fast clip, then saying, 'Now go.' And while I'm (or any one of her friends, I'm sure) telling my stuff, she'll interject with these great insights that involve pulling details from a holiday story of five years ago or from something small she's remembered about your extended family, but which is totally relevant. And funny. And comes so easily for her.* "

Attending. Listening. Recalling. Checking in. Interjecting. Giving. Saying. Inspiring. This is the sweet travail of sisters, which comes so easily, doesn't it?

The Sweet Travail of Sisters Is In the Attending Interjecting Recalling and Listening.

28

And So I Was There Early

" *My friend and I share the Disease of Punctuality, which is easily understood by people who have it, and looked at strangely by the rest of the world. You spend a lot of time being 10, 15 minutes early for things, waiting around, always being the first one there, even when it's a pain to do so. It's just a compulsion. She definitely has it and so do I, so often when we're telling a story, there's a chance to say, '. . . and so I was there early . . .' Then the other one says, 'OF COURSE,' because it just is, of course. With the rest of the world I'm always apologizing for getting places early and catching normal people off guard or half-ready. With Ruby, if I'm five minutes early, she'll ask why I'm late. Which I love!* "

What do you love about your best sister or gal pal? Have you told her lately? Why not?

HAVE YOU TOLD YOUR *Gal Pal* LATELY WHAT YOU **LOVE** ABOUT HER?

Why Not?

29 1014

"During college I became linked to five of the most extraordinary women I am sure I will ever meet: my 1014 roommates. Ten-fourteen is the address of our house where we spent late nights learning about what you really should learn while away at college. So, 10/14, or October 14, has become what we consider a national holiday. Every October 14, the coolest wineshop in whatever city we are in can expect to sell a bottle of wine to each of us. As we link together in text messages, e-mails, or phone calls that evening, we lift our glasses to the laughter, the lessons, and the love that made us who we are today. We encourage all the young women we meet to do the same: embrace the sisterhood you cherish and claim a national holiday in its honor."

Linked together: an auspicious metaphor of friendship, isn't it?

We women link together like golden chains. Despite the miles, marriages, careers, or children that demand our best efforts, the links that bond best buddies are indeed the lessons and love that made us who we are today.

As the women of 1014 remind us: Embrace your sisterhood. Proclaim a national holiday. Call them together. Raise a glass. Shout them out. And remind all of the younger women in your life to do the same.

Coming to Kick Your Ass

I don't know my biological sisters, but I have a chosen sister. In my opinion, that makes our relationship even better.

We are on speed dial on all of our telephones and have keys to each other's homes. We share holidays and celebrations, illness and heartache . . . and most important: dog sitting and wardrobes! My family has become hers . . . her family has become mine.

We share many 'girls' vacations,' usually to a beach somewhere, which include consuming lots of her favorite: gin and juice with a salty rim. We are each other's 'wing women' when in unfamiliar territory—whether it be a foreign country or just a bar full of drunk men. She was there and ready to go when I needed to learn to surf to usher in a new decade and 'kick 40s butt' all over the beach. She's been there for just about everything for the last 10 years.

We talk multiple times a day and have a therapy session at least once a week. Some call it 'happy hour,' but it's way more than that.

Two weeks ago my sister had a health scare and had to have surgery. Today, we will face another health issue together as I go with her to the doctor for a biopsy. It will be a long week waiting for the results, but I know that individually we are strong women, but together we are a force to be reckoned with. So, look out, cancer! If you are there, we are coming to kick your ass.

Watch out, world. When sisters stand shoulder to shoulder, they are a force to be reckoned with.

WHEN SISTERS STAND SHOULDER TO SHOULDER, WATCH OUT, WORLD.

Not Quite as Sharp

My best friend and I secretly share a little saying. It makes its way into almost every conversation. And—unfortunately—it is almost always applicable.

For my birthday a few years ago she game me an adorable, funky, vintage-y, little metal flip-top notepad with a dandy little pen that slips into the casing on the side. On the front was an illustration of a middle-aged rather attractive woman. The words above and below read: 'My memory is not quite as sharp as it used to be. . . . Also, my memory is not quite as sharp as it used to be.'

From that moment on, the phrase has given us much comic and literal relief. When we can't remember the single reason we called: 'Sorry, sistah. My memory is not quite as sharp as it used *to be.' When we forget to call when we say we will: 'You know, my memory is not quite as sharp ...' When we start to tell the same story again and again: 'OK, my memory is not ... you know ...'*

Knowing that both our memories are not quite as sharp as they used to be is comforting; knowing that we can embrace our aging with great wit is priceless. So is she. ”

Embrace your friends, sisters, and sistahs for all that they do to comfort you in the glorious reality of growing. And getting older. Wiser. And so much better as a result.

Also, did we mention that women are all getting older? Wiser? Better?

Thought so.

32 Nice and Simple

My best friend and I send each other e-cards with jokes or happy wishes at least once a month.

The best relationships are rather nice and simple, aren't they? There when you need them. Happy most of the time. Reciprocal. Reasonable. Fresh. And sustainable.

Why not begin—or simply revive—a joy-producing (yet highly manageable and low in cost) ritual with one of your best buds? Like an e-card. Or a real card. Or even a postcard. What could be nicer and simpler?

And because happy wishes are almost always reciprocated, you'll be getting a great return on your investment, no doubt.

33 The Notebook

"My best friend and I keep a notebook that we share. One week I will have the notebook and I fill it with motivational quotes and stories, or funny jokes. I will slide it in her mailbox and she will keep it for a week and fill it with photos, stories, stamps, stickers, drawing, clippings . . . and return it to me the following week! We have been going back and forth forever. It's not because we don't get to see each other often or anything like that; it's because when we do find something interesting or cool that we think the other would like, we want to share it with the other person. It's such a fun way to enjoy each other and our close friendship."

Good old-fashioned handwriting. Cutting and pasting. Stickers. Photographs. And a dime-store spiral notebook. Put it all together and it results in something rather cool, don't you agree?

Like these friends, you too—no matter your age or income or zip code—can begin an ever-emerging keepsake that will keep you and your best friends nice and close. No texting or Internet or cell phone required. Just good old pen and paper.

What a novel idea.

34 Sharing Her Pain

" *When my best friend was a teenager, she gave her son up for adoption. I met her in college soon after and ended up in the same city for a while after graduation. On his birthday, we'd hole up in her bedroom and talk about his age, how big he must have been by that year, what toys he probably liked to play with, what he looked like now. When we moved away from one another, we still did this by phone, having the same conversations, each year bringing new specifics. Sharing her pain continues to bond us more than all of the good times we have together.* "

"Sweet is the voice of a sister in the season of sorrow."
—Benjamin Disraeli

"SWEET IS THE VOICE
OF A *Sister*
IN THE SEASON
OF *Sorrow*."

—Benjamin Disraeli

35

Sisters' Catering

" We are four sisters who are very close but live all over the country. So whenever one of our kids graduates from high school we all come and cook and cater the big open house. It was our oldest sister Kate's idea. She said she really wanted us all to come and the only way she could ensure that we'd really come was to invite us to help her cater the event. She said, 'You're all better cooks than we could ever order out for!' So we all flew down and helped. And our oldest sister showed up with silk-screened white aprons on which were printed the theme, 'Sisters' Catering,' and hand-drawn illustrations of each one of us—they look just like us. We'll wear these aprons until all our kids have graduated. And so many people at these open houses will say to us, 'Is your business in town here?' and we'll laugh. 'No, we're really the sisters!' So the idea of sisters' catering not only gets us together, but the best thing is that it gives *us time together that we don't have otherwise: without our kids, we're shopping and cooking, and we have a full day or two together, just sisters doing what we all love.*"

   Budget-friendly? No question. But more important, the way these sisters have come together to celebrate each other—and the offspring who make them proud—is the most valuable gesture of all. No question.

Celebrating Each Other
Is the *Most* Valuable
Gesture Of All.

36

Drop Everything

I have a ritual with my best friend, Bridget. If there is new information to gossip about or rumors or anything related to us, we IM or text each other with the saying 'oooooooookay.' When we get that message we have to drop everything—whatever we are doing—so we can grab our phones and talk about the updated information or latest news.

These women are on to something. Something superhealthy, actually. According to Terri Apter and Ruthellen Josselson, authors of *Best Friends: The Pleasures and Perils of Girls' and Women's Friendship*, one of the first things women do when they get overstressed about work or family is let go of friendships with other women. Yet there is strong empirical evidence that those satisfying bonds with others—especially other women—can significantly reduce the stress and thus the illnesses in our lives.

Drop everything. And DO something, right now, to nurture your bestie relationships. Maybe take a tip from the very oooooooookay friends: Develop a simple system for staying connected. More routinely. No matter what else is on your plate. Just drop everything. And give her a call or text. You'll be not only wiser but healthier too.

37 Gotta Minute?

"I've got this one sister who I'm not sure how I ever lived without. I did live without her for the first 30 years of my life. But for the past 13 years she's been, well, indispensable. Valuable. Treasured. All that important stuff you would look for in a sister if you could pick your own. Which, I guess, I did.

We have some things in common like young kids, political views, husbands, parents, in-laws, and careers long gone, and new ones on the horizon now that our nest is empty during the day. But the beauty of our sisterhood lies in the REALLY important stuff we share like:

The belief that not much on earth can beat a good peanut butter and bacon sandwich. Maybe a BLT. She and I can share a beet salad and then a beet pizza and if they made beet cake . . .

Also, when our kids were really little we could call each other and say, 'Gotta minute?' and it was understood based on the tone of the other person's voice and/or the sound of the crying in the background, that you just say, 'Of course. Go.' And you listen and support and encourage and not judge. Even when the other person whispers into the phone, crying, 'I kinda hate them right now.' Or, 'I feel like I'm going to lose my mind. What's so friggin' hard about using the potty, a toothbrush, getting in the tub, eating, dressing, doing homework, practicing piano?!'

A true sister listens. We listen. There is absolutely positively no judging ever. It never occurs to either one of us. How amazingly valuable and rare. "

We couldn't agree more.

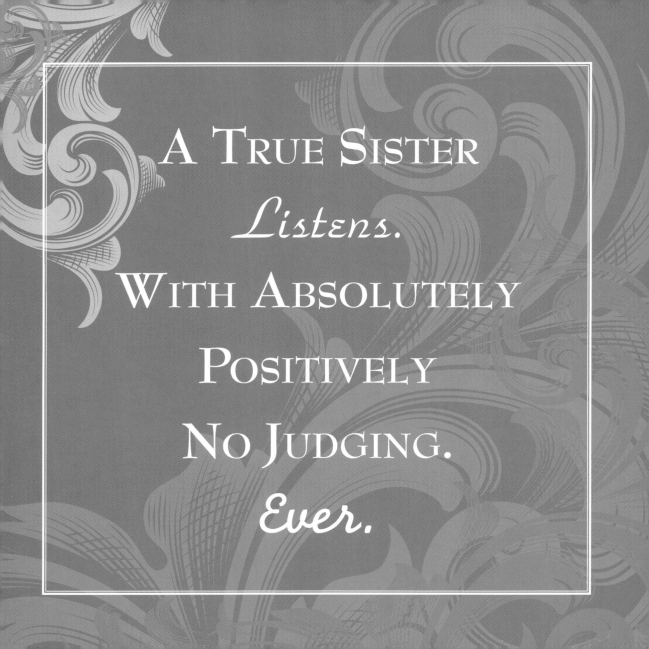

A TRUE SISTER

Listens.

WITH ABSOLUTELY

POSITIVELY

NO JUDGING.

Ever.

38

Destination Sisters

" My five sisters and I have found it harder to keep in touch as
we each head out in to the world and leave our childhoods behind.
Some of us are married, some starting families, getting first jobs,
and even finishing college. As a way to bond we all decided that
once each year we would celebrate all of our birthdays at once
by getting together at a destination for a weekend! We've been
to Vegas and many other cities and countries; each trip we are
bonding while forgetting about our hectic schedules. We plan to
carry on this tradition for many years to come. "

The destination for these sisters? Happiness. Longevity. And everything that comes from knowing that you have taken the time and made the decision to stay connected.

Forget the excuses. When you decide to sustain your sisterhoods, nothing—not schedules or kids or college or careers—will get in your way. Nor should it. Because sustaining traditions, research shows over and over again, makes for joyful individuals and stronger families. Those, sisters, are destinations at which all hope to arrive.

39

Are You Tweezing Me?

" My sister really likes to tweeze out body hair, especially hair on legs. So when we were growing up she was always tweezing her arm hair and leg hair out. And not only did she take care of her extra hair but mine also. Almost every time I was watching TV in the living room with my sister she would start tweezing my leg hair, just like monkeys grooming each other. That was our everyday ritual. I miss her and need her because my leg hair is really long now because I don't get to see her as much. "

Like our long-ago ancestors (think apes), the trust of sisters is revealed in the mundane and selfless acts of tending to each other. Although you might prefer razor to tweezer, consider how everyday rituals bring you and your best "girl" together, side by side, to care for and be cared about. Without question. Without keeping track. No tweezing required.

EVERYDAY Rituals
AND ACTS OF TENDING
TO EACH OTHER
BRING FRIENDS
TOGETHER
forever and ever.

40

Who Is Ed?

" My sisters and I often answer each other's questions, on purpose, with words that make no sense. And that's how our cards are written to each other too. And for birthdays, we never wrap presents. We just put the gift in a plastic bag or a brown bag and we just throw it at them because it's like, 'Whatever. See if I care it's your birthday.' We act like it doesn't affect us at all, but really we care a ton. And the best part is that the present is usually addressed to and from some man's name. Or one time the gift was addressed to 'Frog. To Frog, From Jerry.' And inside the card it'll say something that makes no sense like, 'Do you like corn?' or 'Where are my shoes?' or 'You are a dog.' And all the letters are written backwards in little kid handwriting. With your left hand. On a recent baby shower card to me from one of my sisters it said, 'The red dragon flies at 0800. You are stupid.' The best is at Christmastime when we're passing out presents and *someone's like, 'Who is Ed?' and the other person has to say, 'Oh, that's Sarah.' Everyone gets so annoyed. But we have so much fun together, all the time.*

Although it might make no sense to *you* why these sisters find great joy in frogs, dogs, and stupid flying red dragons, they'd say: That's exactly the point (stupid)! Because they don't care. Nor should they. Their idiosyncratic ritual of nonsensical notes makes a whole lot of sense to them. And, it would be applauded loudly by relationship researchers.

You see, these sisters have put the fun back in their family by creating their own secret world of corn, caring, and 0800. They are models of how to create energy in one of their most cherished relationships: among sisters.

Why not introduce and sustain playful "Ed" to your gals? "Who's Ed?" He ate the dragon who sat on the frog. Love, Jerry.

And, by the way, where *are* my shoes? Duh.

41

A Windfall of Whisks

"With six sisters, my life has been incredibly full and blessed. Even now that we're all grown and have lives and families of our own, we are as close as ever. For example, we will often independently pick out and send the same birthday card to the birthday girl; she'll receive five of the same card! And then there was the sister who received 12 different whisks for her birthday, chosen independently by each of us because at one time she mentioned she didn't have a whisk in her kitchen. These little things reflect the special love and relationships we share, transcending over 50 years. And the comfort found in being loved so deeply, each giving us the self-confidence to be the women we are today."

Isn't it lovely when the women you like the most in your life simply know what you need? What you love? What you adore?

Because, as you surely recognize: 12 whisks + five matching cards + 50 years of loving little symbolic gestures of closeness = A very precious, comforting, and priceless sisterhood.

42 Knock Three Times

"When my younger sister Elise and I were growing up we shared a room and had a set of bunk beds. I always slept on the top. I don't remember how it originated but we started a secret language between just the two of us. Different knocks mean different things. Back then, three knocks meant 'Are you still awake?' and/or 'Do you want to talk?' Two knocks meant 'yes,' a pound with the fist meant 'no,' and one knock then rolling your fingers meant 'good night.' Even today—many decades later—when we are both at home or are traveling together we will sleep in the same room and use our secret knocking language! It brought us closer back then and continues to do the same for us now."

The beauty of sisters? Simply knowing each other's language.

The Beauty of "*Sisters*" Is Knowing Each Other's Language.

43 It's Just Called That

"I have a group of women friends; we first met during a parenting class long ago. After months of getting together with the kids we said how about we go out together, just the mothers? I remember coming home after the first night and saying, 'Oh my God! They are all so interesting.' Because before that night none of us ever had a full conversation with each other. Our kids had our attention. So now it has morphed into this thing called 'Moms' poker night.' But there's no poker. It's just called that.

I get together with these great women and there is no reading a book, no doing anything but showing up. I just get to talk to people who are having a similar experience, like, 'Are your boobs leaking? Mine are leaking!' Or 'I lost all the baby weight but I'm still shaped like a pyramid. What's up with that?' And after

Moms' poker night, I come home really happy. My husband is so happy too because I'm almost always wanting to have sex when I get home! Sex after poker night. He's very encouraging of it.

Ever notice how powerful sharing similar experiences can be? Like these women, sharing stories about our own experiences, and listening in return, is one of the best and most satisfying parts of creating sisterhood.

And it's not just all for fun. Sharing stories serves an important function in our relationships. Because stories are the way we frame our personal experiences (Bochner, 2002). According to researchers, women often *build* their friendships around the simple act of listening to others' stories (Fox, Gibbs, & Auerbach, 2006). And then they bond emotionally through validating and accepting, as the stories unfold.

Guess story time isn't just for kids anymore.

44 Pearl Points

" At approximately 4 a.m., near the end of a long and lonely first semester of graduate school, seven of my classmates and I became 'sisters,' a full-fledged secret sisterhood. We spent as much time studying for finals as we did laying out the 'rules' of our sisterhood and it was the energy of this bond that got me through one of the most rigorous few months of my life. I am the 'president' because I, admittedly, can 'act' very serious about our rules, making the whole thing even funnier. I even wrote an inaugural address. We keep minutes of our meetings. And we decided right away that if we wanted to be really close, we should haze ourselves. So, for instance, we each must wear pearls on a certain day of the week, even if we are in sweatpants. Failure to do so results in a loss of 'pearl points,' which can only be earned back in two ways: (1) by planning the next fun event or (2) by an act of kindness toward a *sister. If a sister is ever in need, for help with writing, to combat loneliness, or if she needs someone to bring her books because she is ill, we are there, in the bonds of sisterhood. If I reveal more, though, I might get impeached. Divulgence of secrets of the sisterhood is grounds for expulsion.*"

The bond of sisterhood is—quite simply—fabulous.

45 Little Things Like That

When I lived in a different state far away for a few years, I'd call each of my sisters while I was driving home from work. And this was after most of us would be texting each other all day! I think we're all really good at remembering details in each other's lives. We'll follow up and ask, 'Hey, did you ever resolve that issue with so-and-so?' Or, 'How did you feel about this today?' Little things like that.

For most of us, a healthy and loving relationship is a big thing in our life. Because we are social beings, we thrive on being close to and loved by others. Have you stopped to reflect, though, on the fact that our relationships are really a result of—day after day—the little things. Like the daily chats. The catching up. The checking in. The "How are you feeling today?"

DO take a moment to recognize—right now—how your best friends, those women we call "sisters," are those with whom we share a lot of little things. It is the accumulation of those little moments that makes our relationships the substantial presence they are in our lives.

THE ACCUMULATION

OF THOSE *Little* MOMENTS

IS WHAT MAKES

Sisterhood

SUBSTANTIAL.

46 Oh My Gosh

" *My sisters and I laugh all the time. We call each other if we see something funny. Funny accents, funny clothes. It's so mean. But we laugh. We laugh at family relatives and our own parents. We'll call each other and be like, 'You will not believe what Aunt Lois just did.' Or 'Oh my gosh, you won't believe what Mom just did!' We think it's funniest when people are doing something that they think is so normal and it's not at all normal to us. It's really common to hear one of us say, 'Oh my gosh, I'm going to pee.' I've wet my pants so many times with my sisters when we're laughing! We can read each other's faces. Sometimes when we're in public, we'll have to NOT look at each other because we know we're going to start laughing at something.* "

The evidence is rich and conclusive: Laughter is an elixir. A beloved medicine. A reducer of stress hormones (think cortisol and epinephrine). And oh my gosh, sisters, it's totally free! DO get some. Soon!

47 On a Little Plate

My sisters and I (there are four of us) would always leave out M&M's on a little plate, one for each year you're turning. Happy birthday, sister!

Celebrate your sisters. Your friends. The women in your life who make your presence feel like it matters. Time and again.

And why wait for a big day like a birthday? DO find new large and small ways to celebrate any day. Because being celebrated for just *being* is such a treat, no matter your age.

FIND BOTH miniature

AND **Grandiose**

WAYS TO CELEBRATE

YOUR *Sisters.*

48

Here's the Deal

I have three sisters and we all really care about each other and each other's feelings. It must have started long ago because when we were little, Maureen said, 'Okay, when we get married someday, here is who is going to be each other's maid of honor': Barbara is going to be Maureen's is going to be Kara's is going to be Jillian's, etc. And we stuck with the deal! It made it so nice because when two of us got married around the same time we were like, 'No problem. We've had this decision made from when we were little.'

Rules are key in healthy relationships. Especially in those long and satisfying ones, because they create the conditions for successful interaction. Like cars at an intersection, knowing what is expected— implicitly or explicitly—helps you and your "sisters" navigate the present and anticipate each other's needs and desires for the future.

DO encourage rules to emerge and discuss them openly. By doing so, you might just avoid the uncomfortable pileups that so often happen when we—watch out!—simply don't know the rules of the road.

49 Stick It

"For some reason my sisters and I, long ago, started taking all our fruit stickers off our fruit and sticking them on the inside door of our refrigerator. Still today it's completely covered in fruit stickers. It's kind of funny because when we go to their homes and open the door to the fridge you can maybe fit one more on the bottom. I remember when I was in college I would try doing that; I'd take a sticker off my apple and stick it on the fridge. But of course my roommates were upset because they'd be like, 'No, that doesn't belong there!' Now, when I see a sticker on a piece of fruit I want to take it off and put it inside the door of our refrigerator! I always think of my sisters when I see a fruit sticker."

What makes you think of your sister? And when that something triggers a memory of her or a time in your past, do you let her know? Why not?

DO reach out and remind one of your "sisters"—that woman in your life who sticks with you like red on an apple through the tough and the tumble—that you are thinking of her.

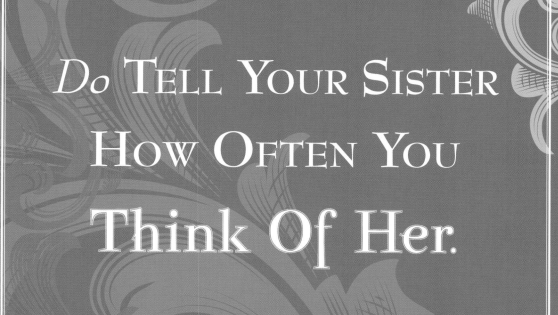

Do Tell Your Sister
How Often You
Think Of Her.

Knock-Down-Drag-Out

" I have seven sisters! To this day, whenever we see each other we have a water fight. One of my favorite memories is from my dad's funeral a number of years ago. My dad died suddenly from a heart attack and afterwards—I don't even know who started it—we went back to the family farm and we had a water fight. So instead of having a traditional mourning funeral, we had this great water fight. And today, no matter what the occasion, somehow one of my sisters sneaks up with a water balloon. It's a knock-down, drag-out water fight!

Saturate your relationships—especially those with the women who make your family life both wildly wonderful and a wee bit wacky—with spunk. Like the eight sisters in this story, DO create ways for introducing zestful traditions into your gatherings. Give them a splash of something new.

And if someone gets irritated with your surprising actions, just look innocent and declare, "But she started it!"

Saturate Your Relationships With Surprise.

51 Holding Our Own

"My sisters and I have a saying that goes like this: 'I'm a Horton girl. I hold my own.' Although there are three boys in my family, who are all really nice and successful, all us girls were very focused on our careers; we are very strong-willed and driven. My dad named all the boys after himself, and he'd tell you the boys were his favorites. So we sisters developed this bond because we've all gone through difficult times and come out stronger. We're Horton girls. We hold our own. We laugh now because we see our own daughters getting into it! Without a doubt, there is a firm tradition in my family of strong women who make a difference."

Who is the woman in your life who has made a difference? A strong difference? Made you stronger and tougher and cheered you on when you thought you couldn't hold your own? Think about her, and then think about what you are DOing to pass it along to another female in your life.

52 Nutty-Putty-JJ-Crinklecups

"*My mom had five girls in eight years. We sisters all have the letter 'A' as the second letter in our first name: Madeline, Kathryn, Janice, Barbara, and Lana. So we'd shorten our names to LA or JA. We'd also—and have continued to—make up funny rhyming nicknames for each other, like bloody-belly-barbie-Barb or nutty-putty-jj-crinklecups-Jane. We'll still get letters from a sister and it'll say, 'Love, BA.' Or 'Love, MA' or one of those silly nicknames.*"

What's in a name? Quite a bit more than you'd expect, according to our research. Nicknames and other private expressions simply bring people together. They say, "I know you like no one else!"

So, if you've been trying to forget or have avoided bringing to light your "sister's" nutty-putty-crinklecups nickname, you should reconsider. Sharing secret words can remind you of your past. Of good times. Of your long history. Or they'll at least make you laugh, which is nothing but good for everyone.

Whatcha waiting for, wig-wallie-Wanda?

Soul Sister

"My older sister, by six years, Kari has played many roles throughout my life. As a young child, Kari was my parent-sister, often telling me what or what not to do in ways that were not always well received. Kari then grew to be my role model-sister: telling me to get over the boy who just broke my heart or to toughen up on the basketball court. In high school, Kari was my confidant-sister: helping me navigate my high school years and guiding me through the college search process. In college, Kari became my best friend-sister. Although she lived hundreds of miles away, our daily phone calls, e-mails, and mail kept me going. She always knew the right thing to say and just how to say it. Kari's personality was incredibly strong and confident but so caring. In January of 1998 (my junior year of college), Kari's life was taken in a car accident. It was to be a joyous time in her life as her *husband had just received a promotion and they were planning a move. She was in the car with her daughter, Mikael, who was then two. I will never, ever forget receiving that devastating phone call from my brother saying, 'Kari passed away' and the agony that followed with losing my sister and best friend. The next few weeks were spent waiting, as Mikael recovered from a serious brain injury due to the accident.*

Today, Kari is my guiding light and soul-sister. I live my life as I think she would have lived hers—as a mother, wife, daughter, sister, friend, and co-worker. I continue to pray that I may model my life after hers and anticipate the day we can be together again. And, until then, I keep her memory alive when I indulge in a Minnesota State Fair pronto pup (or two) every year, smell the new lilac blooms in the spring, and treasure the extraordinary in every day as she so wonderfully did. "

Treasure all of your sisters. In every day, moment, and way.

TREASURE *All* OF
YOUR *"Sisters."*
IN *Every Day,*
MOMENT, AND *Way.*

54 Meltdowns

" *My mom and three of our family's best women friends go out to dinner at least once every weekend. We call our get-togethers 'meltdowns' because they are at the end of the week and it is a way for all of us to wind down and relax with each other as we talk about work, school, family, and our goals. To help, we always order a new kind of wine; we're into trying new wines and sharing our different wine discoveries with each other. Our weekly 'meltdown' is such an important part of our relationship because it keeps us connected.* "

What makes women's relationships so beautiful are the discoveries of each other—and thus ourselves—in our momentary, mundane, daily, weekly, and whenever conversations.

DO develop a ritual—then protect and preserve it—with the women with whom you love being connected. For over time, it's the accumulation of those moments that adds up to something most magical: a sisterhood of support.

55 A Better Sister

" *One of the things I've been working on these days is being a
better sister. I have one sister who is the complete opposite of me.
I decided to call her for her birthday and say, 'Your present is that
I'm going to be a better sister.' So I dug in my files and pulled out
all the postcards from different places like New York or wherever,
and I stuck them right in the kitchen. So when I think of my sister
I can pop a stamp on one and send it. When I think of something
like, 'Oh, I want to tell so-and-so . . . ,' I can just jot it down and
send it. Everyone gets e-mails, but snail mail is not in vogue
anymore. So that's a new thing I'm implementing this year: being
a better sister.* "

What could you do to be a better sister or friend? What could you do to
reignite a relationship gone stale or sour?

Even if time has elapsed and conflicts have eroded your patience for her unique personality, what's the harm is digging deep in your soul and finding even the simplest way—in vogue or not—to be in touch. To be within reach. To be nicer. To be a better sister or friend. You won't regret being better. And neither will she.

BE a better sister.

Bibliography

Apter, T., & Josselson, R. (1998). *Best friends: The pleasures and perils of girls' and women's friendships.* New York: Three Rivers Press.

Bochner, A. P. (2002). Perspectives on inquiry III: The moral of stories. In M. Knapp and J. Daly (Eds.), *The handbook of interpersonal communication,* 3rd ed. (pp. 73–101). Thousand Oaks, CA: Sage.

Fox, M., Gibbs, M., & Auerbach, D. (2006). Age and gender dimensions of friendship. *Psychology of Women Quarterly, 9,* 489–502.

Goodman, E., & O'Brien, P. (2000). *I know just what you mean: The power of friendship in women's lives.* New York: Simon & Schuster.

Hankinson, S. E., Colditz, G., Manson, J. E., & Speizer, F. E. (2001). *Healthy women, healthy lives: A guide to preventing disease from the Landmark Nurses' Health Study.* New York: Fireside.

Leach, M. A., & Braithwaite, D. O. (1996). A binding tie: Supportive communication of family kinkeepers. *Journal of Applied Communication Research, 24,* 200–216.

Taylor, S. E., Klein, L. C., Lewis, B. P., Gruenewald, T. L., Gurung, R. A. R., & Updegraff, J. A. (2000). Female responses to stress: Tend and befriend, not fight or flight. *Psychology Review, 107,* 411–429.

Wood, J. T. (1982). Communication and relational culture: Bases for the study of human communication. *Communication Quarterly, 30,* 75–84.

Also by Carol Bruess and Anna Kudak

What Happy Couples Do
Belly Button Fuzz & Bare-Chested Hugs—
The Loving Little Rituals of Romance

What Happy Parents Do
Ninety-Three Cents and a Little "Humpty Dumpty"—
The Loving Little Rituals of a Child-Proof Marriage